FENG SHUI
IN SMALL DOSES

for
WEALTH &
PROSPERITY

Feng shui in small doses for
Wealth & Prosperity.
by
Lillian Too
© Konsep Lagenda S/B

ISBN 983 - 9778 - 11 - 0

Also in this series

*Romance,
Love & Marriage*

*Work
and Career*

*Published by
KONSEP BOOKS
Malaysia
April 2000*

For Wealth & Prosperity

1

The secret of prosperity feng shui is creating the essence of wealth chi in your home by always protecting against secret poison arrows, and activating wealth corners with powerful symbols of good fortune

2

Good wealth luck exists only where there is adequate protection against killing chi, which causes bad feng shui. This is an important first step. So start by being defensive in your practice of feng shui.

3

Looking out for the sources of killing energy requires you to develop a natural awareness of all things that are sharp, pointed, straight, angular or hostile, that seem to be hitting at your entrances.

4

Watch out for heavy beams above you when you eat, or when you work. They create killing chi inside your home or office. Move out from under such beams if you wish to prosper.

5

Protect your main door against straight roads and driveways, which should not point directly at the door. Place a Pa Kua mirror above the door outside directly facing the straight road.

6

Use the same Pa Kua mirror if the pointed triangle of a roofline is directly facing your front door. Or when a single tree, a lamp post or a tower is sending killing energy straight at your main door.

7

Tall and imposing buildings, especially the edge of such building can be dangerous poison arrows. Such sources of killing chi should be blocked from view with trees & high walls.

8

If it is possible to do so, use another door or entrance, and close the afflicted main door permanently. This is a better and more lasting remedy to the threat posed by big poison arrows.

9

When changing door directions, use your auspicious KUA directions, and work out the new Flying star natal charts of the house. Door direction s offer the potential for creating excellent wealth luck

10

KUA directions are based on Chinese birth years and gender. Those born before Feb 4th must adjust for the Chinese year by deducting one year from their birth year. This uses the <u>solar calendar</u> of the Chinese year.

11

Under the Chinese <u>lunar</u> calendar the New Year dates vary from year to year. Using the solar calendar is also acceptable but those with access to the lunar calendar can countercheck the conversion date.

12

To obtain your KUA number, add the last two numbers of your year of birth. Keep adding until you obtain a single digit. For men deduct this from 10 and for women add 5 to this digit. The result is your KUA number.

13

If you are a male born on 3rd Jan 1946, your KUA number is based on 1945. So add 4+5=9. Then 10-9=1 so your KUA # is 1. If you are a woman your KUA # is 9+5=14 and 1+4=5. Your Kua # is 5.

14

With your KUA number you can identify your most auspicious wealth direction. This is known as your <u>sheng chi</u> direction. Check your sheng chi from the Table of directions on the next page

15

SHENG CHI DIRECTIONS

KUA #	Sheng chi
1	Southeast
2	Northeast
3	South
4	North
5 males	Northeast
5 females	Southwest
6	West
7	Northwest
8	Southwest
9	East

For Wealth & Prosperity

16

Memorize your sheng chi as this is your success direction. This compass method is based on one of the most powerful feng shui formulas and is known as Eight Mansions formula.

17

Only those with KUA numbers 3, 4, 5, 2, and 8 can use their sheng chi for the main door. Orientate your main door to directly face your sheng chi without getting hit by any poison arrows.

18

Those with KUA numbers 1 and 9 will benefit from homes with main doors that face north or south.. Those with KUA numbers 6 and 7 will benefit from main doors that face southwest or northeast.

19

If your main door is
in the garage, use
the orientation of the
house (instead of the
door) to tap your
sheng chi. This means
your sheng chi
direction is facing
the road - the source
of maximum yang
energy.

20

If neither your main door nor the general orientation of your house faces your sheng chi, look for a secondary door that does and use that door to come in and out of your house. Direction is always taken inside facing outwards.

21

Your wealth luck will always be threatened if your main door is hit by killing chi even though it may be facing your sheng chi direction. So always make sure that nothing is hitting at or symbolically hurting your main door !

22

The universal wealth
sector of any building,
house or room is said to
be the southeast corner.
Energizing the wood
element of this sector is
believed to enhance the
wealth chi of the home.
Place anything made
of wood here.

23

Energize the southeast with healthy and lush green plants. The energy of fresh young plants in this corner is very auspicious as it symbolizes the trigram sheng and the energy of sheng chi, both of which signifies growth.

24

Artificial silk plants can also represent the wood element and they work just as well if they look real and are kept clean. In the same way fake flowers are also acceptable from a feng shui perspective.

25

Dried flowers should never be used in the decoration of the home since they signify excessive yin chi. The use of potpourri is OK but not recommended unless they are placed in the toilets.

26

When the Southeast
corner of a home is
missing due to its
shape, wealth luck
tends to be temporary
and short-lived.
Place a large healthy
plant in the corner
and install a mirror
on one wall to
compensate

27

Missing SE corners cause a lack of opportunities to improve your income luck. A possible solution is to shine a bright light directly at the wall, which symbolically creates good yang chi.

28

Placing a mirror on one wall near the SE sector creates "virtual space" inside the mirror. If you use this solution to correct a missing SE corner make sure the mirror does not reflect a bed, a toilet, a door or the kitchen.

29

A mirror in the dining room creates excellent prosperity because symbolically it doubles the food served. Mirrors should always reflect auspicious objects. Reflection of water brings income luck.

For Wealth & Prosperity

30

Never place mirrors
to reflect the stove in
the belief it doubles
food being cooked.
Reflecting a naked
flame is dangerous
and can cause
accidents. Meanwhile
mirrors in bedrooms
that reflect the bed
leads to infidelity.

31

Fish signify richness
and abundance.
Thus keeping carp
goldfish and the
lucky arrowana in
the home brings
wealth luck. So keep
an aquarium or
display fish symbols
in ceramic or metal.

32

To jump start your wealth luck place an aquarium with bubbling water in the southeast of your living room. Keep nine goldfish (one of which is black) to signify the fullness of heaven and earth.

33

Hang a faceted
crystal ball, about an
inch in diameter, on
a window in the SE
corner. This captures
yang sunshine, which
create auspicious
rainbows laden with
sheng chi. Very
auspicious.

34

Place an image of any of the Chinese Gods of Wealth on a table facing the main entrance door. My personal favourite is <u>Tsai Shen Yeh</u> who sits on a tiger. Or you can display <u>Kuan Kong</u> who also brings wealth luck.

35

A very popular wealth symbol is the three-legged toad. I have several in my home. I place them everywhere in the living room looking at the main door. They are better placed low than on high tables.

36

To find the Wealth or
SE corner of the house
always use a good
compass. Stand in the
center of the house or
room and take your
compass bearings.
Take three readings
to be accurate.

37

In feng shui, water
symbolizes wealth but
it must flow in an
auspicious direction
and be correctly
placed. If it is placed
incorrectly it can
cause loss and
breakup of
marriages.

38

*Always differentiate
between big and
small water. Big
water is natural.
Correctly tapping the
luck of big water
brings awesome
prosperity. Small
water is artificial.
This too can be very
auspicious.*

For Wealth & Prosperity

39

A river is big water. Orientate your house to let the main door face the river so that opportunities for making money can ripen successfully. If this is impossible open a door which faces the river.

40

A lake or pond is big water. Capture its fantastic wealth luck by making certain you can see it from inside your house, or from your main door. Try installing mirrors that reflect a view of the water.

41

Big or small water should not be located on the right hand side of the front door (inside looking out). While it brings prosperity luck, this orientation cause the Patriarch to develop a roving eye.

42

If your home faces a river make sure it flows in a way that brings you prosperity. So houses that face primary directions - north, south, east and west - rivers should flow from left to right.

43

Houses whose main door face secondary directions, northwest, northeast, southwest or southeast - should have waterways flow pass the front door from right to left. (Standing at the door, looking out.)

44

Irrespective of whether water is natural or artificial, water should always flow towards the house rather than away. Remember this when you build ponds and waterfalls.

45

Fountains placed in front of entranceways do not create money luck unless its water is flowing towards the house. If it does not, the water chi of the fountain is dissipated.

46

Rivers with branches flowing into them just before flowing past your house, are said to bring awesome money luck. It symbolizes many sources of income. If there are three branches the luck is magnified further.

47

Rivers that flow in a straight line towards the front door of the house have the same negative effect as a T junction. The straightness of the river is like that of a road. It becomes a harmful poison arrow.

48

Water that flows from a higher ground towards the house from the front bring bad luck. It is said to be unbalanced. Waters that flow from higher ground from behind or from the side of the house bring good luck.

49

Water that flows towards the house broad and leaves narrow after flowing pass the main door is said to have brought gold to the house. This is auspicious water

50

The best kind of natural water is a river that seems to embrace the house like a <u>jade belt</u>. This brings prosperity for five generations. But water must be clean and clear and slow moving. Fast moving or dirty water brings no benefit.

51

The absolute best way of enhancing wealth luck is to energize the lucky water stars of the Flying Star natal chart of your house. This is an advanced technique of feng shui that is based on the nine sector Lo Shu grid.

52

Natal charts are
based on the period
when houses get built
or renovated, and on
their orientation. We
are presently in the
period of 7 which
ends on 4th Feb 2004.

53

Recommendations for tapping the water star are for homes built or renovated in period 7. Accurate door orientations produce the natal chart, which identifies wealth bringing lucky water star locations.

For Wealth & Prosperity

54

Main doors that face South(1) between 157.5 to 172.5 degrees have the auspicious water star at the back of the house in the northeast sector. Place a pond or water feature in that part of the house for prosperity luck.

55

Main doors that face South (2/3) between 172.5 to 202,5 degrees have their auspicious water star in the front of the house in the southwest corner. Putting an aquarium here creates wealth luck.

56

Main doors facing North 1 (between 337.5 to 352,5 degrees) have the auspicious water star in the north corner in front of the house. Creating a waterfall here will activate excellent wealth luck.

57

*Main doors facing
North 2/3 (between
352.5 to 022,5 degrees)
have the lucky water
star at the back, in
the Southwest grid.
This is one of the few
houses where placing
water in the SW
brings money luck.*

58

Main doors that face West 1 (between 247.5 to 262.5 degrees) the lucky water star is at the back in the southeast sector. Water placed here brings good income. It also works if water is in the SE corner of the living room.

59

Main doors that face West 2/3 (between 262.5 to 292 degrees) your lucky water star is in the northwest sector to the right of the front door. A water feature here brings enormous money luck but could hurt the marriage.

60

Main doors facing
East 1 (between 067.5
to 082,5 degrees) have
the auspicious water
star in the north east
corner towards the
left of the front of the
house. An artificial
waterfall here brings
excellent wealth luck.

61

With main doors that
face East 2/3 (between
082.5 to 112.5 degrees)
the lucky water star
is in the Southwest
corner at the back of
the house. Energize
with an aquarium or
any suitable water
feature.

62

With main doors that face Southwest 1 (between 202.5 to 217.5 degrees) potential wealth luck resides in the North at the back of the house. Enhance with water features - small waterfalls stocked with gold fish and terrapins

63

With main doors that face Southwest 2/3 (between 217.5 to 247.5 degrees) prosperity potential lies in the South to the left of the front. Activate with water - ponds, pools or aquariums and watch yourself grow rich.

64

*Main doors facing
Northeast 1 (between
022.5 to 037.5 degrees)
have their auspicious
water star in the east
sector next to the
front door on the
right. Strengthen this
with a strategically
placed pond.*

65

With main doors that face Northeast 2/3 (between 037.5 to 0675 degrees) the auspicious water star has flown to the back. It is located in the west sector. Energize with an aquarium.

66

With main doors that face Southeast 1 (between 112.5 to 127.5 degrees) wealth potential is in the east sector on the left of the main door. Water features here crystallize your wealth luck.

67

With main doors that face Southeast 2/3 (between 127.5 to 157.5 degrees) you must activate the water star in the west sector at the back so best to energize the west corner of the living room.

68

Main doors facing.
Northwest 1 (between
292.5 to 307.5 degrees)
have auspicious
water star in the
center of the house. If
you place an
aquarium here it will
bring wealth luck to
every member of the
family.

69

With main doors that face Northwest 2/3 (between 307.5 to 337.5 degrees) the auspicious water star is in the center of the house which is also the luckiest spot for other types of luck. Place water here for wealth.

For Wealth & Prosperity

70

When you activate prosperity luck with water remember never to overdo the size of the water feature. When there is an excessive amount of moving water it may overflow and create imbalance..

71

An important tip on the activation of the auspicious flying water star is that you can activate both the small chi and the big chi of water. Big chi refers to the whole house. Small chi applies to the sector of each room.

72

*An important symbol
of wealth luck is the
'golden coin', which
are round with a
square hole in the
center. This
represents heaven
and earth luck. Place
three in your wallet
to create money chi.*

73

Tie three of these Chinese coins with red thread to imbue them with the precious yang energy and then stick them onto important files and Invoice books to enhance sales turnover in your business.

For Wealth & Prosperity

74

Wear "coin" jewelry
made of real gold
and set with a
diamond
to simulate the
Chinese coins. Both
men and women can
wear nine of these
golden coins to
attract excellent
money luck.

75

Another personal adornment, which attracts wealth luck, is the arrowana ring or necklace. If you are in business or you play the stock market the arrowana ring will be particularly helpful.

76

A powerful feng shui tool for improving income luck is the merchant sailing ship, symbolizing wealth brought by wind and water. Place a painting or a model of such a ship facing inwards in your house or office.

77

Display your sailing ship after filling its deck with fake gold ingots (real gold is even better if you can afford it) and place it on a coffee table sailing inwards from your sheng chi direction.

78

You must make sure there are no cannons on your sailing ship since this brings tiny slivers of poison arrows into your house. Remove any cannons and transform your ship from a warship to a merchant ship.

79

You may, if you are greedy like me, place several ships in your home, one in each room thereby symbolically turning your home into a rich harbour. This brings you many different sources of income.

80

Use the SUN trigram in your office. Two solid yang lines above a broken yin line. SUN signifies the wind, which brings prosperity by scattering seeds that take root, germinate, grow and blossom.

81

The golden rice bowl is an excellent potent symbol of asset accumulation especially when energized by the breadwinner of the family. Displaying such a bowl in the dining room is most auspicious.

For Wealth & Prosperity

82

Wealth luck must be protected at all times. One feng shui ritual that preserves your wealth is the protection of the family rice urn. Never allow it to get empty. Replenish when half full.

83

The family rice urn is always covered, always made of an 'earth' material, and always kept hidden away in a storeroom. Family wealth is seldom displayed, as this attracts jealous spirits who cause it to be lost.

For Wealth & Prosperity

84

Placing a red packet
containing real
money deep inside
the rice urn will
safeguard the
family's wealth and
assets. Adding a red
packet with money
each lunar New Year
causes family wealth
to multiply.

85

During the lunar New Year a popular tradition amongst the Hokkiens is to display the pineapple fruit which indicates that 'good luck is coming' or has arrived at your doorstep.

For Wealth & Prosperity

86

A popular feng shui tradition during the lunar New Year is the display, consumption and exchange of juicy, succulent mandarin oranges. Oranges symbolize 'gold' because the word for oranges is <u>kum</u> which mean gold.

87

Specially cultivated lime trees dripping with hundreds of ripe succulent fruit which have turned into a beautiful golden colour bring excellent prosperity luck when displayed flanking the front door. This signifies your home is filled with fruit about to be harvested.

For Wealth & Prosperity

88

A cardinal rule during the start of any year is that red should be the dominant colour worn and displayed. Red symbolizes precious yang energy and at this time of the year, yang energy brings exceptional good luck for the rest of the year.

89

Hanging red lanterns during the first fifteen days of the New Year is vital for attracting yang chi into the house. It is even better if auspicious calligraphy using the word 'fook' which means luck is painted onto these lanterns.

For Wealth & Prosperity

90

Another source of the auspicious yang chi is loud noise created by a lion dance. The clashing of cymbals and beating of drums attracts accumulation of good energy that will last through the year. You might want to have a lion dance this coming new year !

91

A major symbol of
abundant prosperity is
the red bat. The Chinese
believe that when bats
nest in your home you
are about to become
seriously rich. If you
cannot wait for them to
come on their own you
can always hang a
painting with lots of
red bats in your home.

92

Wealth feng shui is created when you keep a money plant in your home. This is referred to as the 'jade plant' because its leaves resemble pieces of cabochon jade.

93

If you want to be rich, and to stay rich, never have artificially stunted trees in your home. These bonsai plants are such bad news that I strongly recommend against keeping them.

94

Cactus and other
spiky plants also
cause unlucky chi to
cast shadows on your
general financial
well being. Keep these
unfriendly plants at
the edge of your
homes thereby
turning them into
guardians.

95

If you want prosperity never place the stove in the northwest of your kitchen. In addition to other manifestations of bad luck this also cause you to lose your wealth. In feng shui terms this creates <u>fire at heavens gate.</u>

96

Let your rice be cooked and your water be boiled using energy that comes from your wealth direction. Place your rice cooker and your electric kettle with their plugs pointing to your sheng chi if you want prosperity.

97

When sitting at the
dining table, make
sure you are facing
your sheng chi or
wealth direction. Use
a compass to ensure
this. But make sure
you are not being hit
by inauspicious
energy around you.

98

Bad energy hits you
if you sit directly
under a toilet
located on the floor
above. How can you
have wealth luck
when you eat your
meal under a toilet ?
Change your seat
and move the dining
table immediately.

99

Prosperity luck becomes afflicted if your main door is located under a toilet on the upstairs floor. This is difficult to overcome. Money leaks out of the house steadily. Try shining a light upwards to 'raise the chi'.

100

Never sit directly facing a door when you eat, and especially when that door leads to the toilet. This will severely curtail your money luck. Move the chair a little out of the way.

101

Do not sit with exposed bookshelves behind you. In addition to hurting your health such shelves also cut into your finances. I personally know several very rich tycoons who lost a great deal of their wealth within three years of having exposed shelves behind them.

102

Sleeping feng shui is important for creating prosperity luck. Try to sleep in a bedroom, which is located in your sheng chi direction, and have your head (when you are lying down) pointed to the sheng chi direction.

103

You must always try to sleep with a solid wall behind you. So while it is OK to move your bed at an angle to the wall to tap the sheng chi direction, don't do it if the angle gets too pronounced.

104

Don't sleep under an exposed overhead beam and try to avoid getting 'hit' by the sharp edge of a protruding corner of your bedroom. These block prosperity luck.

105

Do not sleep with feet or head pointing to the door into the bedroom, as this will subject you to harmful chi. And do not sleep with two doors on either side of you. Use a screen to block one of the doors.

106

A bed which has a headboard gives good support when you sleep. A rounded headboard is better than a fancy one. The headboards of brass beds do not offer sufficient support.

107

It is preferable to have a solid wall behind your bed but if there is a WC on the other side of the wall because your toilet is located there you should move your bed away.

108

Improve sales turnover by installing wall mirrors on the two side walls of your shop. This doubles your customers and your business. Do not let mirrors be placed directly facing the entrance as this creates disappearing chi, which is bad for business.

109

Placing a wall mirror next to the till can enhance the profit of your shop. This symbolically doubles the money collected. Just make sure that the mirror is large enough. Using a puny little mirror will be ineffective.

110

It is not conducive to
good feng shui if your
cash register is placed
directly facing the
door. This causes
income to leak out. It is
also not good to place
the cash register too
near the entrance. The
most auspicious place
to collect money is deep
inside the shop.

111

Placing a bell on the entrance door to your shop creates good yang energy each time a customer walks in enhancing the chances of their spending money in your shop. But you must complement this by hanging coins tied with red thread deep inside the shop.

For Wealth & Prosperity

112

Another business feng shui tip is to hang hollow bamboo stems energized with red thread high above the cash register. These should be placed at an angle such that the space between them is longer at the bottom than at the top.

113

Stick three coins tied with red thread on your cash register, your cash box and your Sales Book. Use sticky tape to do this. This will make an immediate improvement to your sales turnover.

114

Develop the prosperity signature. On financial documents always sign your name, starting and ending with a firm upward stroke. Make sure there is not even a hint of a back or downward stroke at the end.

115

As we approach the year 2004 when the period of 8 starts, start incorporating the number 8 into your cards, addresses and important numbers. 8 is a lucky number which means coming prosperity but for 20 years beginning in 2004 the number 8 is doubly lucky.

For Wealth & Prosperity

116

Please note that while 7 is very lucky now, this ends when period of 8 begins in February 2004. After that date, 7 becomes a violently unlucky number so you have four years to get rid of the 7.

117

Also protect your wealth luck from the deadly <u>annual five yellow star.</u> Find out where it resides in your home each year and hang a 6 rod windchime there to overcome its bad vibes.

118

The deadly five
yellow is in the
NORTH in 2000; in
the Southwest in
2001, in the East in
2002 and in the
Southeast in 2003.
Don't let the 5 yellow
destroy your rich
lifestyle.

119

Don't allow the 'three killings' to spoil your fun either. Note its direction each year and ensure you never sit with your back to it. Otherwise you will get stabbed in the back, get cheated and suffer losses.

120

The direction of the 3 killings is summarized below.

In the years of the…	The 3 killings is in the:
ox, rooster, snake	EAST
boar, rabbit, sheep	WEST
monkey, rat, dragon	SOUTH
dog, horse, tiger	NORTH

For Wealth & Prosperity

121

The final warning is
that you must always
respect the <u>Grand Duke
Jupiter.</u> If you disturb
or confront him with
renovation, excessive
noise and digging, you
will lose money,
position and power.
Never sit facing the
direction where he lives
each year.

122

The Grand Duke
Jupiter's location

YEAR	HOME OF GRAND DUKE
2000	east/southeast from 112.5 to 127.5 degrees
2001	south/southeast from 142.5 to 157.5 degrees
2002	south from 172.5 to 187.5 degrees
2003	south/southwest from 202.5 to 217.5 degrees

123

Lucky numbers are 1 and 6. When these two numbers combine with 8, the good luck is awesome. The number 9 is an independent number indicating distant prosperity. 9 has the power to magnify the bad luck of bad numbers and the good luck of good numbers.

For Wealth & Prosperity

124

Bad luck numbers
are the two "earth"
numbers – 2 and 5.
These numbers
indicate bad luck
under the flying star
system. But when 2
and 5 occur with 8,
the three numbers
together spell
excellent luck.

125

Those with KUA 7 are enjoying good fortune during the period of 7. Their run of good luck will last until Feb 2004. Those with KUA 5 and 8 will enjoy excellent good fortune during period 8, from Feb 2004 to 2024.

For Wealth & Prosperity

126

Create a wealth vase.
Fill it with three
coins in a red packet,
soil taken from a rich
man's house, & seven
types of semi precious
stones to reflect this
period of 7. Add one
precious item each
year. Keep the vase in
your bedroom.

127

For protection against financial loss wear a double fish symbol. Or a small gold dragon. When using the dragon in your corporate logo do not enclose or imprison the dragon with borders. Let him fly.

128

Display a dragon tortoise sitting on a bed of coins and ingots in the east to symbolize both short and long term prosperity luck.

Dedication

*for
my family
With love*

FENG SHUI
on line at

www.worldoffengshui.com

www.lillian-too.com

www.lilliantoojewellery.com

EMAIL the author at
Feng shui@ lillian-too.com